THE
Sopranos™
THE OFFICIAL
COCKTAIL BOOK

THE Sopranos™

THE OFFICIAL
COCKTAIL BOOK

INSIGHT
EDITIONS

SAN RAFAEL · LOS ANGELES · LONDON

"I'M GONNA FINISH MY DRINK."

TONY SOPRANO
SEASON 2, EPISODE 10

CONTENTS

INTRODUCTION
— 9 —

HOW TO USE THIS BOOK
— 10 —

TOOLS OF THE TRADE
— 13 —

SOPRANOS SIMPLE SYRUPS
— 14 —

MAFIA HITS
— 21 —

NEW JERSEY CLASSICS
— 51 —

FAMILY FAVORITES
— 75 —

CELEBRATIONS AND OCCASIONS
— 115 —

CLASSICS
— 143 —

INDEX
— 156 —

INTRODUCTION

The New Jersey world of Tony Soprano and his soldiers is gray, gritty, and tough—all cement, strip clubs, big sedans, big men. Brown suits, zip-up jackets, St. Christopher medals, chain bracelets. Slicked hair (*amazing* hair), slow smiles, handguns (especially handguns). And we can't forget splashy homes, backyard pools, fancy jewelry, extra lipstick, fur coats. Pasta with marinara, gabagool, steaks and sausages on the grill. And liquor . . . plenty of liquor.

In the world of *The Sopranos*, a friendly drink can seal the deal between bosses and give you a bit of courage before a tough hit. It can be the last thing you ever taste—right before that new hole opens up in your torso. It might warm you during a long night in Pine Barrens (if only!). A good drink will fill your glasses during both a toast at Vesuvio and a night at the Bada Bing! bar.

We've tried to capture a bit of that *The Sopranos* cocktail magic throughout these pages, featuring plenty of whiskey drinks in a nod to Tony's favorite spirit, Italian fortified wines, and liqueurs to honor the show's origins, a few callouts to Naples, Paris, and Hollywood—and a distinct New Jersey flair for all.

For these drinks, you'll only need basic barware—shakers, jiggers, rocks glasses, highball glasses. If you want to take a little deeper dive into the art of crafting delicious cocktails, we've got a window into making your own rosemary, raspberry, and cinnamon syrups, as well as a delectable recipe for tomato water.

Although life with Tony Soprano can be heartbreaking, ruthless, and exhausting, it's also gorgeous, gentle, wickedly funny, and delightfully absurd. Either way, you're going to enjoy your stay here even more with a drink in your hand. So, grab your shaker and a glass, stock up on ice, and survey your bar. Salute!

HOW TO USE THIS BOOK

Imagine a cocktail party with your friends, frenemies, one or two weird relatives, and a few neighbors (so they won't complain about the noise you're making). The theme of the party involves *The Sopranos* or gangsters or the mob. You could try figuring out what drinks to fix from an all-in-one guide, or you can use this one, which is exactly what you need.

The book is divided into five parts. Really, it's four parts plus four takes on classic drinks that will pass muster with any boss, even Tony Soprano.

Mafia Hits is all about the rough-and-tumble drink that every soldier and associate will want. These are great sips to put into your guests' hands after you hang up their coats.

New Jersey Classics is another set of cocktails to introduce to your friends if they're scared off by the first set. These are really tasty—perfect for guys and dolls who are more into kicking back.

The third part, Family Favorites, leans into Tony's go-to drinks, with a nod or two to a few family members who enjoy an adult beverage. These drinks should really get the party going, especially for *The Sopranos* connoisseurs in the crowd.

Finally, Celebrations and Occasions is ideal for birthdays, anniversaries, announcements, milestones—you name it. But don't let that stop anyone from creating a reason to drink them, of course!

The last four recipes are Classics. Each of these drinks is a liquid version of kissing the ring. You can't go wrong serving them.

Enjoy them all. What are you waiting for? Get busy!

TOOLS OF THE TRADE

Time to look classy while delivering the goods. Sure, you could use a regular teaspoon while stirring a drink, or a jar with a lid to shake ingredients, but that's not giving the drink the respect it deserves. Live a little and invest in the right tools for the job.

BARSPOON
It's long and thin, has a twisted shape, and is made for efficient stirring.

GLASSWARE
Different types of drinks go best in different types of glasses. A good selection of glassware might include highball, rocks, martini, coupe, margarita glasses, and copper mugs.

JIGGERS
These small cups, attached at either end of the jigger, help measure alcohol before mixing or shaking. The large cup holds 1½ ounces and the small cup holds 1 ounce.

MUDDLER
Use this slim tool to crush mint and other herbs or fruit at the bottom of a glass before mixing in the liquid ingredients.

SHAKER
Try a two-piece version with a small cup that fits into a larger cup for easy shaking or a three-piece version with a cup, a lid, and a strainer.

STRAINER
This sieve fits inside your cocktail shaker—use it to keep ice or other solid chunks from falling into your drink as you pour.

SOPRANOS SIMPLE SYRUPS

Back in the day, a couple of ice cubes and some whiskey in a glass were all you needed to make a drink. Today, everyone is a mixologist or something. But if you're not going to have your whiskey neat, these sweet concoctions will add a little mob flair to your cocktail. They're simple for a reason. With some sugar and herbs mixed with hot water, you can have your drink turned into something special. And what's not to like about that?

SIMPLE SYRUP

1 CUP SUGAR
1 CUP WATER

In a small saucepan, combine equal parts sugar and water. Place the saucepan over medium heat and stir continuously. Keep stirring until the sugar dissolves completely. This usually takes 1 to 2 minutes. Once the sugar is dissolved, allow the mixture to simmer for 1 to 2 minutes. After the sugar is fully dissolved and the syrup has slightly thickened, remove the saucepan from the heat. Let the simple syrup cool to room temperature. Pour the simple syrup into a clean, airtight container. You can use a glass jar or a plastic bottle for easy storage. Simple syrup can be stored in the refrigerator for up to 3 weeks.

HONEY SYRUP

½ CUP HONEY
½ CUP HOT WATER

In a small saucepan, combine the honey and hot water over medium heat, stirring for 1 to 2 minutes until the honey dissolves completely. Allow to cool and transfer to an airtight container. Honey syrup can be stored in the refrigerator for up to 1 month.

BROWN SUGAR SYRUP

1 CUP FIRMLY PACKED, DARK BROWN SUGAR

1 CUP WATER

In a saucepan, combine the brown sugar and water over medium heat. Cook, stirring the mixture constantly, until the brown sugar has completely dissolved, 3 to 5 minutes. Reduce the heat and let it simmer for about 5 minutes, or until the syrup has thickened slightly. Remove the saucepan from the heat and let the brown sugar syrup cool to room temperature. Once cooled, transfer the syrup to an airtight container. Store the brown sugar syrup in the refrigerator for up to 2 weeks.

DEMERARA SYRUP

1 CUP DEMERARA SUGAR

1 CUP WATER

In a saucepan, combine the demerara sugar and water. Heat the mixture over medium heat, stirring constantly, until the sugar is completely dissolved, 1 to 2 minutes. Once the sugar is dissolved, remove the saucepan from the heat and allow the syrup to cool to room temperature. Transfer the demerara syrup to a clean, airtight container. Store it in the refrigerator for up to 2 weeks.

ROSEMARY SYRUP

½ CUP SUGAR

½ CUP WATER

3–4 FRESH ROSEMARY SPRIGS

In a small saucepan, combine the sugar and water. Add the rosemary sprigs to the saucepan. Heat the mixture over low heat, stirring until the sugar completely dissolves, 1 to 2 minutes. Simmer for 1 to 2 minutes to infuse the syrup with rosemary flavor. Remove from the heat and let the syrup cool to room temperature. Strain the syrup to remove the rosemary sprigs. Transfer to an airtight container. Store the rosemary syrup in the refrigerator for up to 1 week.

CINNAMON SYRUP

4 CINNAMON STICKS

1 CUP SUGAR

1 CUP WATER

Combine the sugar and water in a saucepan over low heat, stirring until the sugar completely dissolves, 1–2 minutes.

Remove from the heat and add the cinnamon sticks. Cover and let sit to cool for at least 2 hours. Strain out the solids. Transfer to an airtight container. Store the cinnamon syrup in the refrigerator for up to 1 month.

RASPBERRY SYRUP

½ CUP SUGAR

½ CUP WATER

½ CUP FRESH RASPBERRIES

In a small saucepan, combine the sugar and water. Add the raspberries and heat the mixture over low heat, stirring until the sugar completely dissolves, 1 to 2 minutes. Allow the syrup to simmer for 5 to 7 minutes, mashing the raspberries with a fork to release their flavor. Remove from the heat and let cool to room temperature. Strain the syrup to remove the raspberry solids. Transfer to an airtight container. Store the raspberry syrup in the refrigerator for up to 2 weeks.

MAFIA HITS

Whether you're ready for a whiskey sour, Tony-style, or you need a bit of a pick-me-up from an espresso martini, these cocktails provide a bit of an introduction to the world of *The Sopranos*. Interested? By all means, come on in.

PAULIE WALNUTS OLD-FASHIONED

Whether he's sucking down on ketchup packets with Christopher in the Pine Barrens or lamenting the takeover of Italian cuisine by big American companies, surely one of Tony's most loyal—and aggravating—soldiers deserves a drink every now and then. Our old-fashioned adds a dash of walnut bitters and a walnut garnish in homage to that incident from Paulie's past (TVs, hijacking . . . walnuts?!). Stir up this concoction and raise a toast to the best hair in New Jersey.

---

2 OUNCES WHISKEY

½ OUNCE BROWN SUGAR SYRUP (PAGE 16)

3 DASHES WALNUT BITTERS

WALNUTS, FOR GARNISH

In a mixing glass, combine the whiskey, brown sugar syrup, walnut bitters, and ice. Using a barspoon, stir for about 15 seconds until well chilled. Strain into a rocks glass over a large ice cube. Garnish or pair with a few walnuts.

WHACKED WHISKEY SOUR

"Hi, Jack. Bye, Jack." You know what goes great with a clinking glass of whiskey? Blood splatters. Inspired by Tony and his colleagues' favorite spirit, this frothy take on the whiskey sour adds pomegranate juice in homage to that particular decorating technique. A shaken egg white lends some froth and quiets the bite of the lemon. Just think of it as a silencer for your drink. Tony certainly would.

---

2 OUNCES BOURBON OR WHISKEY

¾ OUNCE FRESHLY SQUEEZED LEMON JUICE

½ OUNCE SIMPLE SYRUP (PAGE 14)

½ OUNCE POMEGRANATE JUICE

1 EGG WHITE

LEMON WHEEL OR MARASCHINO CHERRY, FOR GARNISH

In a cocktail shaker, combine the bourbon, lemon juice, simple syrup, pomegranate juice, and egg white. Shake the ingredients vigorously without ice (dry shake) for 10 to 15 seconds to froth the egg white. Fill the shaker with ice. Shake again, this time with ice, until well chilled, 10 to 15 seconds. Strain the cocktail into a chilled rocks glass. Garnish with a lemon wheel or maraschino cherry—or both.

NEW BLOOD NEGRONI

Tony's "new blood" Davey Scatino might have wished he *wasn't* after the all-night, executive poker game at Shlomo Teittleman's hotel. Instead, Davie might have been happy to hand that title over to our twist on a Negroni, here made with blood orange gin with a blood orange garnish. Tony and his friends like things bloody—and in this case, so do we.

---

1 OUNCE MALFY BLOOD ORANGE GIN

1 OUNCE CAMPARI

1 OUNCE SWEET VERMOUTH

BLOOD ORANGE SLICE OR TWIST, FOR GARNISH

Place a large ice cube in a rocks glass. Pour the Malfy blood orange gin over the ice cube. Add the Campari and sweet vermouth. Stir gently to combine and chill the ingredients. Garnish with a blood orange slice or twist.

ITALIAN HIGHBALL

Infused with a blend of herbs, spices, peels, and flowers that's sweetened and aged, the Italian grape brandy amaro is right at home on Tony and Carmela's bar. Here, our Italian highball blends with ginger beer for an authentic tribute to the land of grapes, sunshine—and mobsters.

1½ OUNCES AMARO

4 OUNCES GINGER BEER

2 DASHES AROMATIC BITTERS, SUCH AS ANGOSTURA

LEMON TWIST, FOR GARNISH

Fill a highball glass with ice. Pour your favorite amaro into the glass. Add the ginger beer and aromatic bitters. Stir gently to combine the ingredients. Garnish with a lemon twist by expressing the citrus oils over the drink and dropping it in.

COGNAC CAPO SANGAREE

Sangaree is like a delightful single-serve sangria in a cocktail glass. Here, we add Cognac and port wine for a warming punch that's perfect for winter. Tony's capos might enjoy this at the bar at Vesuvio, wearing their suits and cuff links, snow falling outside. It's winter, it's New Jersey, it's time to get classy.

2 OUNCES RÉMY MARTIN COGNAC

1 OUNCE PORT WINE

½ OUNCE SIMPLE SYRUP (PAGE 14)

½ OUNCE ORANGE LIQUEUR, SUCH AS COINTREAU OR GRAND MARNIER

½ OUNCE FRESHLY SQUEEZED LEMON JUICE

2 DASHES AROMATIC BITTERS, SUCH AS ANGOSTURA

MARASCHINO CHERRY, FOR GARNISH

Fill a coupe glass with ice to chill and set aside. Pour the Rémy Martin Cognac into a mixing glass. Add the port for depth and flavor. Pour in the simple syrup for sweetness. Add the orange liqueur for citrusy notes. Add the lemon juice to brighten the mix. Add the aromatic bitters for complexity. Stir the mixture gently to combine the ingredients. Empty the ice from the glass, then strain the cocktail into the chilled glass. Garnish your Cognac Capo Sangaree with a maraschino cherry for an elegant finishing touch.

MAFIA MARTINI

"One thing about us wise guys? The hustle never ends." Tony, Paulie, and the crew never get a break. It's handguns, cement blocks, piles of cash, and the occasional garroting. Maybe they should relax once in a while with our Mafia Martini—we've added Lillet in place of vermouth for brightness and maraschino liqueur and blood orange juice for a scarlet blush. Salute!

¾ OUNCE VODKA

¾ OUNCE LILLET

¾ OUNCE MARASCHINO LIQUEUR, SUCH AS LUXARDO

¾ OUNCE FRESHLY SQUEEZED BLOOD ORANGE JUICE

In a mixing glass, combine the vodka, Lillet, maraschino liqueur, and blood orange juice. Add ice and stir the ingredients gently to combine and chill. Strain the cocktail into a chilled martini glass. Garnish with a maraschino cherry.

BAD BLOOD

Tony's world has all kinds of blood—family blood bonds, bad blood between feuding capos, and, of course, the kind that sprays against the car window—or the hotel wall, for that matter. Our tribute to this most sacred fluid comes in the form of our Bad Blood sweet-and-citrusy bourbon cocktail, with scarlet color provided by raspberries and grenadine and lemon juice to keep it tough enough for Tony.

---

6 TO 8 FRESH RASPBERRIES, FOR MUDDLING AND FOR GARNISH

2 OUNCES BOURBON

½ OUNCE GRENADINE SYRUP

½ OUNCE FRESHLY SQUEEZED LEMON JUICE

DASH ORANGE BITTERS

In a cocktail shaker, muddle the raspberries gently to release their juices and flavor. Add the bourbon, grenadine syrup, lemon juice, and orange bitters. Fill the cocktail shaker with ice cubes. Shake the ingredients vigorously for 10 to 15 seconds to chill and combine. Strain the cocktail into a rocks glass filled with ice. Garnish with a couple fresh raspberries.

SMOKED SCOTCH

Cigar smoke swirls around Tony in his car, in his backyard, in the back rooms where he does his business. Evoke some of your own smokiness here by making your own . . . smoke. Here, we've created rosemary smoke, letting it coat a rocks glass and giving your cocktail an earthy, dusky depth.

---

2 FRESH ROSEMARY SPRIGS, 1 SLIGHTLY DRIED FOR SMOKING AND 1 FOR GARNISH

2 OUNCES SCOTCH WHISKY

½ OUNCE DEMERARA SYRUP (PAGE 16)

2 DASHES AROMATIC BITTERS, SUCH AS ANGOSTURA

Start by preparing the rosemary smoke: Take a small, dry rosemary sprig and ignite it using a kitchen torch or an open flame until it begins to smolder and release aromatic smoke, about 5 seconds. Place a rocks glass upside down over the smoldering rosemary to capture the smoke inside the glass. While the glass is smoky, turn it right side up and let the smoke infuse for a moment. Once the glass is well smoked, carefully lift it and set it aside.

Pour the Scotch whisky into a mixing glass. Add the demerara syrup and the aromatic bitters. Fill the mixing glass with ice cubes. Stir the ingredients gently for 20 to 30 seconds to chill and combine. Strain the cocktail into the smoked rocks glass over a large ice cube. Garnish with a fresh rosemary sprig.

THE HITMAN

Dark and dusky, this sweet brown cocktail is our tribute to Tony and his crew's many, many (did we say many?) hits. The Hitman might remind you of the front seats of cars, hotel room floors, hotel room bathtubs, muddy streams in the woods, boats on the Jersey waters, back rooms, front rooms, sidewalks, underpasses. Enough? Probably not. Mix up another Hitman. You've still got time before they arrive.

---

2 OUNCES BOURBON

½ OUNCE AMARETTO LIQUEUR

½ OUNCE COFFEE LIQUEUR, SUCH AS KAHLÚA

2 DASHES ORANGE BITTERS

ORANGE TWIST OR LUXARDO CHERRY, FOR GARNISH

In a mixing glass, combine the bourbon, amaretto liqueur, coffee liqueur, and orange bitters. Add ice and stir the ingredients gently in the mixing glass for 20 to 30 seconds to chill and combine. Strain the cocktail into a chilled rocks glass filled with ice. Garnish with either an orange twist or a Luxardo cherry.

WHACKED LONG ISLAND

Want to get whacked? Probably not. Makes such a problematic hole in your forehead. Want to feel whacked? That's a better idea. This take on a Long Island iced tea can help. A tequila-whiskey-gin-rum–triple sec will knock you back faster than Christopher's handgun. Top it with a couple ounces of cola to take the edge off—or don't.

½ OUNCE BLANCO TEQUILA

½ OUNCE BOURBON WHISKEY

½ OUNCE GIN

½ OUNCE LIGHT RUM

½ OUNCE TRIPLE SEC

½ OUNCE FRESHLY SQUEEZED LIME JUICE

½ OUNCE SIMPLE SYRUP (PAGE 14)

DASH AROMATIC BITTERS, SUCH AS ANGOSTURA

2 OUNCES COLA

LIME WEDGE, FOR GARNISH

Fill a tall glass with ice cubes. In a cocktail shaker, combine the blanco tequila, bourbon whiskey, gin, light rum, triple sec, lime juice, simple syrup, and a dash of aromatic bitters. Fill the cocktail shaker with ice. Shake the ingredients vigorously for 10 to 15 seconds to chill and combine. Strain the cocktail into the prepared tall glass filled with ice. Top off the cocktail with cola. Garnish with a lime wedge.

RISE & CRIME

Frank Sinatra Jr. needs a little pick-me-up after a high-stakes all-night poker game with an angry Silvio. Tony's offer of coffee is very welcome, especially with a little Sambuca splashed in. The anise-flavored liqueur adds a delicious layer of flavor to our decadent sweet coffee with cream. With this brew in hand, Frank will leave the poker table a little more awake—even if he's also leaving a little poorer.

1½ OUNCES SAMBUCA

3 OUNCES FRESHLY BREWED HOT COFFEE

¼ OUNCE SIMPLE SYRUP (PAGE 14)

½ OUNCE HEAVY CREAM OR HALF-AND-HALF

Pour the Sambuca into a heatproof glass or coffee mug. Add the freshly brewed hot coffee. Stir the simple syrup to sweeten. Carefully pour the heavy cream over the back of a spoon to create a layered effect.

ITALIAN ESPRESSO MARTINI

Sometimes New Jersey is just a little snowy, a little gray, a little slushy—and even your zip-up jacket leaves you shivering. Time for a little pick-me-up, espresso martini-style. Here, we add Kahlúa, amaro, and amaretto cream liqueur for a delicious, sweet blend, shaken up with espresso to warm *you* up on your way to your next hit. Happy hunting!

1½ OUNCES VODKA

1 OUNCE COFFEE LIQUEUR, SUCH AS KAHLÚA

½ OUNCE AMARO

1 OUNCE FRESHLY BREWED ESPRESSO, COOLED

½ OUNCE AMARETTO CREAM LIQUEUR

SIMPLE SYRUP (PAGE 14), FOR SWEETENING (OPTIONAL)

COFFEE BEANS OR ESPRESSO BEANS, FOR GARNISH

Fill a cocktail shaker with ice. Add the vodka, coffee liqueur, amaro, espresso, amaretto cream liqueur, and simple syrup to taste, if desired. Shake the ingredients vigorously for 10 to 15 seconds to chill and combine. Strain the cocktail into a chilled martini or coupe glass. Garnish with a few coffee or espresso beans.

ITALIAN WHITE RUSSIAN

Though White Russians actually have nothing to do with Russia (the Russian moniker comes from the inclusion of vodka), Valery and Slava might appreciate this nod to their home country in our twist on this delicious milk shake–like drink. A splash of Italian Sambuca gives it an anise twist, as well as a callout to the Italian mobsters we know and love so well.

1½ OUNCES VODKA

1 OUNCE COFFEE LIQUEUR, SUCH AS KAHLÚA

½ OUNCE SAMBUCA

1 OUNCE CREAM OR MILK

Fill a rocks glass with ice. Pour the vodka, coffee liqueur, and Sambuca into the glass. Top off the cocktail with cream or milk. Stir the ingredients gently to combine.

ESPRESSO & TONIC

"How did we miss out on this? F—king espresso, cappuccino. We invented this shit and all these other c—k suckers are getting rich off it." Paulie keeps it succinct—and profane. Can someone please just get the man a coffee? Or instead, our Espresso and Tonic, which is even better: nutty, a little bitter, a little bubbly. Just what Paulie needs to put him right again.

---

1 OUNCE FRESHLY BREWED ESPRESSO, COOLED

1 OUNCE AMARO

3 TO 4 OUNCES TONIC WATER

LEMON TWIST, FOR GARNISH

Brew a shot of espresso, using an espresso machine or stovetop espresso maker (moka pot). Allow the espresso to cool to room temperature or chill it in the refrigerator for 15 minutes. In a highball or rocks glass filled with ice, combine the amaro, espresso, and tonic water. Gently stir to combine the ingredients. Garnish with a lemon twist.

NEW JERSEY
CLASSICS

Tony's family, friends, and soldiers don't live in a vacuum. They live in *New Jersey*, and this singular place provides the inspiration for this batch of quaffers. From the Pine Barrens Highball (page 55) to Whitecaps Punch (page 64), let these drinks lead you on a Garden State tour, with or without blood splatters.

THE BADA BING!

Sometimes the action at the Bada Bing! is onstage. Sometimes it's in the back room. Either way, the topless club is one of Tony's most regular haunts, and it deserves tribute here in our own shaken concoction. We've used bourbon (or whiskey, if you choose) for a rugged *Sopranos* vibe, a splash of amaretto for a nutty twist, and, for the girls of the Bada Bing!, maraschino liqueur for a bit of sweetness.

1½ OUNCES BOURBON OR RYE WHISKEY

½ OUNCE AMARETTO LIQUEUR

½ OUNCE MARASCHINO LIQUEUR, SUCH AS LUXARDO

½ OUNCE FRESHLY SQUEEZED LEMON JUICE

¼ OUNCE SIMPLE SYRUP (PAGE 14)

LEMON TWIST OR BRANDIED CHERRY, FOR GARNISH

In a cocktail shaker, combine the bourbon, amaretto liqueur, maraschino liqueur, lemon juice, and simple syrup. Add ice and shake the ingredients vigorously for 10 to 15 seconds to chill and combine. Strain the cocktail into a chilled rocks glass filled with ice. Garnish with a lemon twist or a brandied cherry.

PINE BARRENS HIGHBALL

Pine trees, snow, drinks by the fire . . . or maybe pine trees, snow, and a bloodied Russian mobster who can't stay captured? While Paulie and Christopher flounder in their city shoes in the Pine Barrens, you can be mixing up a warming winter-themed highball in the comfort of your own kitchen. Pay a snowy homage to our desperate, chilly pair with a cranberry juice mixer and fresh cranberries for garnish, but don't forget a toast for Valery as well.

---

2 OUNCES WHISKEY

1½ OUNCES CRANBERRY JUICE

1 OUNCE FRESHLY SQUEEZED LIME JUICE

½ OUNCE SIMPLE SYRUP (PAGE 14)

SODA WATER, SUCH AS CLUB SODA OR SPARKLING WATER, FOR TOPPING

LIME WEDGE OR TWIST, FOR GARNISH

FRESH CRANBERRIES, FOR GARNISH

Fill a highball glass with ice. Pour the whiskey into the glass. Add the cranberry juice, lime juice, and simple syrup. Stir gently to combine the ingredients. Top off the cocktail with soda water, such as club soda or sparkling water, to your preferred level of effervescence. Garnish with a lime wedge or twist and a few fresh cranberries.

ATLANTIC CITY MARGARITA

Tony likes to bet and bet big. We do, too. We've raised the stakes here with premium tequila and an extra-bitter flavor from blue curaçao. Mix this up and sip it at the roulette table in Atlantic City with Tony and the crew. Win big, have another, put your chips down again—lose it all. Time to shake up another margarita—or two.

---

2 OUNCES PREMIUM SILVER TEQUILA

1 OUNCE ORANGE LIQUEUR OR TRIPLE SEC

1 OUNCE FRESHLY SQUEEZED LIME JUICE

½ OUNCE BLUE CURAÇAO LIQUEUR

½ OUNCE SIMPLE SYRUP (PAGE 14)

LIME WHEEL, FOR GARNISH

MARASCHINO CHERRY, FOR GARNISH

In a cocktail shaker, combine the premium silver tequila, orange liqueur, lime juice, blue curaçao liqueur, and simple syrup. Fill the shaker with ice. Shake the ingredients vigorously for 10 to 15 seconds to chill and combine. Fill the prepared margarita glass with ice cubes. Strain the margarita mixture into the glass. Garnish with a lime wheel and a maraschino cherry.

JERSEY TOMATO MARTINI

"When the Jersey tomatoes are in season, you can't keep these New York guys away." Vito Spatafore might appreciate our Jersey tomatoes, here in a tomato water martini. This clear juice strained from fresh, ripe (Jersey) tomatoes is full of bright tomato flavor and requires minimal preparation. Our Vito-style cocktail is the perfect icy accompaniment to a hot summer's day.

---

4 TO 5 MEDIUM, RIPE TOMATOES (ANY VARIETY)

FINE-MESH STRAINER OR CHEESECLOTH

MEDIUM SIZE BOWL

2 OUNCES VODKA OR GIN

1 OUNCE DRY VERMOUTH

1 OUNCE TOMATO WATER

CHERRY TOMATO, FOR GARNISH

FRESH BASIL LEAF, FOR GARNISH

Wash and chop the ripe tomatoes into small pieces, removing any stems or tough cores. Place the chopped tomatoes in a fine-mesh strainer or wrap them in cheesecloth. Set the strainer or wrapped tomatoes over a bowl to catch the liquid. Let the tomatoes sit at room temperature for a few hours or overnight, allowing the juice to drip into the bowl. Gently press down on the tomatoes to extract more juice, if needed. Once you have collected enough tomato water, discard the remaining tomato solids. Store the tomato water in a sealed container in the refrigerator for up to 3 days.

Pour the vodka into a mixing glass. Pour in the dry vermouth and tomato water. Add ice and stir the ingredients gently in the mixing glass for 10 to 15 seconds to chill and combine. Strain the cocktail into a chilled martini glass. Garnish with a cherry tomato and a basil leaf.

THE JERSEY DEVIL

Is the Jersey Devil haunting the Pine Barrens? Does this mythic creature need a drink? Perhaps a warming concoction of apple liquor, cranberry, and ginger beer? Its feet might be as frozen as Chris's and Paulie's—this wintry mixture might help take their minds off the cold, hunger, and . . . fear of what's out there in the Jersey wilderness.

---

2 OUNCES APPLE BRANDY OR APPLE-FLAVORED VODKA

1 OUNCE CRANBERRY JUICE

½ OUNCE FRESHLY SQUEEZED LEMON JUICE

¼ OUNCE SIMPLE SYRUP (PAGE 14)

2 OUNCES GINGER BEER

APPLE SLICE, FOR GARNISH

FRESH CRANBERRIES, FOR GARNISH

In a cocktail shaker, combine the apple brandy, cranberry juice, lemon juice, and simple syrup. Add ice and shake vigorously for 20 seconds or until well chilled. Strain into a tall glass with ice. Top up the cocktail with ginger beer. Garnish with an apple slice and a few fresh cranberries.

PINE BARRENS TONIC

Pine trees, snow, pine trees, snow, geese, snow, Paulie's shoe, snow.
Our Pine Barrens tonic is full of bracing wintry flavor—in this case, piney
rosemary syrup you can make yourself (it's delicious). A juniper bite from
the gin and citrus from the fresh lime juice combine to make a drink that
will wake you up—even if you did spend the night in an old van.

---

2 OUNCES GIN

½ OUNCE FRESHLY SQUEEZED LIME JUICE

½ OUNCE ROSEMARY SYRUP (PAGE 16)

TONIC WATER, FOR TOPPING

FRESH ROSEMARY SPRIG, FOR GARNISH

LIME WHEEL, FOR GARNISH

Fill a highball or Collins glass with ice cubes. Add the gin,
lime juice, and rosemary syrup. Stir the ingredients gently in
the glass to combine. Top up the cocktail with tonic water.
Garnish with a fresh rosemary sprig and a lime wheel.

WHITECAPS PUNCH

Caviar dreams on the Jersey Shore—that's what Tony offers Carmela when he brings her on a surprise visit to Whitecaps, their potential vacation house. The only problem? It's not actually for sale. Actually, it's not a problem for Tony, and nothing a giant wad of cash won't fix. You can capture some of those caviar dreams, too—even if you're currently lacking in giant wads of cash. Mix up this fruity rum punch, take it out on the porch, and channel some of that Jersey Shore relaxation.

---

1 OUNCE WHITE RUM

1 OUNCE COCONUT RUM

2 OUNCES PINEAPPLE JUICE

1 OUNCE FRESHLY SQUEEZED ORANGE JUICE

½ OUNCE GRENADINE SYRUP

ORANGE SLICE, FOR GARNISH

MARASCHINO CHERRY, FOR GARNISH

In a cocktail shaker, combine the white rum, coconut rum, pineapple juice, orange juice, and grenadine syrup. Fill the shaker with ice. Shake the ingredients vigorously for 10 to 15 seconds to chill and combine. Strain the cocktail into a tall glass filled with ice. Garnish with an orange slice and a maraschino cherry.

NEW JERSEY SUMMER

New Jersey summers are sticky, humid, and hot. On a sultry night, Tony likes to head to Welsh Farms for a triple blueberry sundae. He might also want to mix up our spiked Arnold Palmer. It's simple, really: just tea, lemonade, and—because we're in Tony's world—a hefty slug of bourbon. Add a lemon wheel to the frosty glass for garnish and enjoy it with your blueberry sundae.

---

2 OUNCES BOURBON

1 OUNCE ICED TEA

1 OUNCE LEMONADE

LEMON WHEEL, FOR GARNISH

In a cocktail shaker, combine the bourbon, iced tea, and lemonade. Add ice and shake vigorously for 20 seconds or until well chilled. Strain into a rocks glass with fresh ice. Garnish with a lemon wheel.

JERSEY STORMS

Tony and Carmela are drinking white wine, but a Jersey-style dark 'n' stormy (in our version, with whiskey) would've been the perfect drink for the cozy meal Tony has with the family at Vesuvio during the big rainstorm. Making sure to use ginger beer instead of ginger ale is crucial—the fermented ginger beer adds an extra layer of spice. Punch it up with fresh lime juice and raise a glass to the small moments with family that are good.

---

2 OUNCES WHISKEY (BOURBON OR DARK RUM)

4 OUNCES GINGER BEER

½ OUNCE FRESHLY SQUEEZED LIME JUICE

LIME WHEEL OR WEDGE, FOR GARNISH

Fill a highball glass with ice. Add the whiskey, ginger beer, and lime juice. Stir gently to combine the ingredients. Garnish with a lime wheel or wedge.

GARDEN STATE PUNCH

Tony's iconic Jersey drive from the Lincoln Tunnel is bridges, grit, gray skies, truckyards, cigar smoke, and a meaty hand on the wheel. It's a love letter to the Garden State. You can write your own mash note with our Garden State Punch—the ultimate recipe with a mix of spirits and several kinds of juice. A bit of club soda adds a pop of fizz.

1½ OUNCES VODKA

2 OUNCES CRANBERRY JUICE

1 OUNCE FRESHLY SQUEEZED ORANGE JUICE

½ OUNCE FRESHLY SQUEEZED LEMON JUICE

½ OUNCE SIMPLE SYRUP (PAGE 14)

1 OUNCE CLUB SODA OR SPARKLING WATER

FRESH CRANBERRIES, FOR GARNISH

ORANGE SLICE, FOR GARNISH

In a cocktail shaker, combine the vodka, cranberry juice, orange juice, lemon juice, and simple syrup. Add ice and shake to chill the ingredients. Strain into a tall glass filled with ice. Top off the cocktail with the club soda. Garnish with fresh cranberries and an orange slice.

JERSEY SHORE SUNRISE

Ah, the sunrise over Jersey. It's been a long night—a lot of poker, a lot of talk, a lot of booze. Here's a pick-me-up for you: a screwdriver, with some orange juice for vitamin C and some vodka for the hair of the dog. Drizzle in some grenadine for a lovely red color—just like the sunrise.

---

2 OUNCES VODKA

4 OUNCES FRESHLY SQUEEZED ORANGE JUICE

½ OUNCE GRENADINE SYRUP

MARASCHINO CHERRY, FOR GARNISH

ORANGE SLICE, FOR GARNISH

Fill a tall glass with ice cubes. Add the vodka and orange juice. Slowly pour in the grenadine syrup over the back of a spoon or by drizzling it down the side of the glass. Do not stir the cocktail; let the grenadine settle at the bottom. Garnish with a maraschino cherry and orange slice.

FAMILY
FAVORITES

From the Uncle Junior (page 90) to Carmela's
Lillet Spritz (page 89), these cocktails pay homage to
Tony's wide circle of family, like-family, and like-family-but-
we'll-still-whack-you-if you-rat. And we haven't forgotten
the big guy himself. The Tony Negroni (page 102) and
Tony's Nightcap (page 113) are here, too—his faves.

SOPRANOS MARTINI

Gin? Vodka? Forget it. Brown liquor is the drink for Tony and his friends.
Shake up a shot of whiskey, a citrus kick from triple sec and lime, and
some cranberry juice for a true *Sopranos* martini—blood color and all.

---

2 OUNCES WHISKEY

½ OUNCE TRIPLE SEC

½ OUNCE FRESHLY SQUEEZED LIME JUICE

1 OUNCE CRANBERRY JUICE

LIME WEDGE OR TWIST, FOR GARNISH

In a cocktail shaker, combine the whiskey, triple sec, lime juice, and
cranberry juice. Fill the shaker with ice. Shake the ingredients vigorously
for 20 to 30 seconds to chill and combine. Strain the cocktail into
a chilled martini glass. Garnish with a lime wedge or twist.

WILD WHISKEY BOULEVARDIER

It's Christmas Eve at Vesuvio and Tony has 50 grand's worth of sapphires for Carmela and a neat Wild Turkey in his hand. Mix some of that holiday cheer with Campari and sweet vermouth and twist an orange peel on the rim for a Tony-style boulevardier. This cocktail calls out Tony's Italian heritage, too, as it's a variation on the Negroni, a popular Italian drink. Add a friendly bathroom beating and call it a very merry *Sopranos* Christmas.

1¼ OUNCES BOURBON OR RYE WHISKEY

1 OUNCE CAMPARI

1 OUNCE SWEET VERMOUTH

ORANGE TWIST, FOR GARNISH

Fill a mixing glass with ice. Add the bourbon, Campari, and sweet vermouth. Stir the ingredients for 20 to 30 seconds to chill and combine. Strain the cocktail into a chilled rocks glass over a large ice cube. Garnish with an orange twist by expressing the citrus oils over the drink and dropping it in.

SOPRANOS BOURBON BRAMBLE

Brambles can be made with gin, but Tony would probably appreciate this version made with bourbon. Blackberry liqueur is dark, fruity, and warming, revived here with lemon juice and further sweetened by a slosh of simple syrup. Sweet like summer, perfect for sipping in the backyard with Tony B. Just don't forget that wet washcloth for your head.

---

2 OUNCES BOURBON

**1 OUNCE BLACKBERRY LIQUEUR,
SUCH AS CRÈME DE MÛRE**

1 OUNCE FRESHLY SQUEEZED LEMON JUICE

½ OUNCE SIMPLE SYRUP (PAGE 14)

FRESH BLACKBERRIES, FOR GARNISH

LEMON SLICE, FOR GARNISH

In a cocktail shaker, combine the bourbon, blackberry liqueur, lemon juice, and simple syrup. Fill the cocktail shaker with ice cubes. Shake the ingredients vigorously for 10 to 15 seconds to chill and combine. Strain the cocktail over ice in a rocks glass. Garnish with fresh blackberries and a lemon slice.

TONY'S OLD-FASHIONED

When Tony slides onto a stool and rests his arms on the bar with a big sigh, he's probably going to ask for a whiskey. A nice single malt. And always on the rocks. Mix up a classic with a nod to Tony's favorite spirit, and don't forget the ice. The big guy's going to thank you when you slide this frosty glass across the bar toward him.

---

2 OUNCES SINGLE MALT SCOTCH WHISKY

½ OUNCE SIMPLE SYRUP (PAGE 14)

2 DASHES AROMATIC BITTERS, SUCH AS ANGOSTURA

2 DASHES ORANGE BITTERS

ORANGE PEEL, FOR GARNISH

In a mixing glass, combine the whisky, simple syrup, and aromatic and orange bitters. Fill the mixing glass with ice. Stir the ingredients for 20 to 30 seconds to chill and combine. Strain the cocktail into a rocks glass over a large ice cube. Express the oils from a strip of orange peel over the drink and then drop it into the glass.

GRAPPA SOUR

Wanting to be nice to Janice, Tony buys them both a bottle of Nonino Picolit after dinner at Vesuvio ("Remember Ma with the bone? Sounded like half-price day at the liposuction center.") Thanks for that image, Janice.) You might want to cut grappa's burn with our mixture. It might not assuage your guilt—nice try, Tony—but it could help you forget it.

---

2 OUNCES GRAPPA

¾ OUNCE FRESHLY SQUEEZED LEMON JUICE

½ OUNCE SIMPLE SYRUP (PAGE 14)

1 EGG WHITE

3 DROPS AROMATIC BITTERS, SUCH AS ANGOSTURA

LEMON TWIST OR WEDGE, FOR GARNISH

In a cocktail shaker, combine the grappa, lemon juice, simple syrup, and egg white. Shake vigorously without ice (dry shake) for 15 to 20 seconds. Add ice and shake again until chilled. Strain the cocktail into a chilled coupe glass. Garnish the cocktail with 3 drops of bitters and a lemon twist or wedge.

THE BIG GUY

Sometimes the big guy likes something a little sweet at the end of a long, murderous day. Is that such a problem? Made with a one-to-one honey-to-hot-water ratio, a delicious honey syrup can take care of that craving, along with a splash of amaretto for a little taste of the home country. Shake this one up with your choice of bourbon or Tony's favorite Scotch.

---

2 OUNCES BOURBON OR SCOTCH WHISKY

½ OUNCE AMARETTO LIQUEUR

½ OUNCE FRESHLY SQUEEZED LEMON JUICE

¼ OUNCE HONEY SYRUP (PAGE 14)

2 DASHES AROMATIC BITTERS, SUCH AS ANGOSTURA

LEMON WHEEL OR CHERRY, FOR GARNISH

Fill a cocktail shaker with ice. Add the bourbon, amaretto liqueur, lemon juice, honey syrup, and aromatic bitters. Shake the ingredients vigorously for 10 to 15 seconds to chill and combine. Strain the cocktail into a chilled rocks glass filled with ice. Garnish with a lemon wheel or cherry.

CARMELA'S LILLET SPRITZ

"Something wrong, Carm?" Yes, something's wrong—Carmela doesn't like priests who like to play it close to the line. A Lillet spritz might bolster her up instead when she eviscerates Father Phil—as he deserves. This fortified wine mixes beautifully in a cocktail—here, elderflower liqueur and fresh grapefruit juice provide light, citrusy flavors, with tang and bubbles from a hefty pour of seltzer.

---

2 OUNCES LILLET

1 OUNCE ELDERFLOWER LIQUEUR, SUCH AS ST-GERMAIN

1 OUNCE FRESHLY SQUEEZED GRAPEFRUIT JUICE

1 OUNCE SODA WATER

ORANGE OR GRAPEFRUIT SLICE, FOR GARNISH

Fill a wineglass or large glass with ice. Add the Lillet, elderflower liqueur, and grapefruit juice. Stir gently to combine the ingredients. Top off the cocktail with soda water. Garnish with an orange or grapefruit slice.

UNCLE JUNIOR

Uncle Junior will take a curaçao if you don't mind. He'll even buy one for
Tony, even though the guy's sitting in his own living room. Maybe our
mixture of gin, herbal curaçao, and lemon juice will help him sort his
complicated feelings about the attempted hit on Tony. Or he could pray
with Father Phil. On second thought, Junior, just take the curaçao.

---

2 OUNCES GIN

1 OUNCE BLUE CURAÇAO

1 OUNCE FRESHLY SQUEEZED LEMON JUICE

½ OUNCE SIMPLE SYRUP (PAGE 14)

LEMON TWIST OR WHEEL, FOR GARNISH

In a cocktail shaker, combine the gin, blue curaçao, lemon juice, and
simple syrup. Add ice to the shaker and shake vigorously for
10 to 15 seconds to chill and combine. Strain the cocktail onto a large ice
cube in a rocks glass. Garnish with a lemon twist or a lemon wheel.

GOLD CHAIN

Tony's gold chain necklace (with a St. Anthony's medal, of course) is one of the big guy's signature pieces. We've paid tribute here with our riff on the gold rush cocktail, essentially a whiskey sour with honey in place of simple syrup. Adding a bit of the amaro liqueur Fernet-Branca gives this cocktail an Italian twist that Tony is sure to appreciate.

---

2 OUNCES BOURBON WHISKEY

¾ OUNCE FRESHLY SQUEEZED LEMON JUICE

½ OUNCE HONEY SYRUP (PAGE 14)

¼ OUNCE FERNET-BRANCA

LEMON TWIST OR WHEEL, FOR GARNISH

In a cocktail shaker, combine the bourbon whiskey, lemon juice, honey syrup, and Fernet-Branca. Shake the ingredients vigorously for 10 to 15 seconds to chill and combine. Strain the cocktail into a chilled rocks glass filled with ice. Garnish with a lemon twist or wheel.

AMERICANO SOPRANOS

An Americano normally combines Campari, rich vermouth, and the bite of sparkling water. Our Americano would be more at home on a table at The Bada Bing! because we've replaced the sparking water with high-proof bourbon or whiskey. This cocktail isn't for sipping in the sun at a Milanese café. Instead, toss it back, put your jacket on, and head out into the New Jersey night. That's where you belong.

1½ OUNCES CAMPARI

1½ OUNCES SWEET VERMOUTH

**1½ OUNCES HIGH-PROOF BOURBON
OR RYE WHISKEY**

ORANGE TWIST OR SLICE, FOR GARNISH

In a mixing glass, combine the Campari, sweet vermouth, and bourbon. Add ice and stir the ingredients for 20 to 30 seconds to chill and combine. Strain the cocktail into a chilled rocks glass filled with ice cubes or a single large ice cube. Garnish with an orange twist or slice.

ITALIAN AMERICAN

Tony, his family, and his capos are Italians first, Americans second. Or is it the other way around? That's a question without an answer, which is why we haven't even tried with our dual-heritage cocktail. Instead, we've blended that most American of spirits, bourbon, with warm, nutty Italian amaretto. Cheers! Salute! Or is it the other way around?

---

2 OUNCES AMARETTO LIQUEUR

1 OUNCE BOURBON

¾ OUNCE FRESHLY SQUEEZED LEMON JUICE

½ OUNCE SIMPLE SYRUP (PAGE 14)

DASH AROMATIC BITTERS, SUCH AS ANGOSTURA

LEMON TWIST, FOR GARNISH

COCKTAIL CHERRY, FOR GARNISH

In a cocktail shaker, combine the amaretto liqueur, bourbon, lemon juice, simple syrup, and aromatic bitters. Add ice and shake the ingredients vigorously for 10 to 15 seconds to chill and combine. Strain the cocktail into a chilled rocks glass filled with ice. Garnish with a lemon twist and cocktail cherry.

SOPRANOS SPEAKEASY SOUR

Dark, a little sticky, and a little tense, the bars and back rooms of New Jersey are Tony's constant backdrop. Our take on a typical whiskey sour is a little dark as well, with demerara syrup subbing in for simple syrup, and a bitter bite from the Aperol. A red wine float finishes it off—a reminder of the business often decided over those sticky tables.

---

2 OUNCES BOURBON

1 OUNCE FRESHLY SQUEEZED LEMON JUICE

½ OUNCE DEMERARA SYRUP (PAGE16)

¼ OUNCE APEROL

½ OUNCE CABERNET RED WINE

ORANGE TWIST, FOR GARNISH

In a cocktail shaker, combine the bourbon, lemon juice, demerara syrup, and Aperol. Fill the shaker with ice. Shake the ingredients vigorously for 10 to 15 seconds to chill and combine. Strain the cocktail into a rocks glass filled with ice. Carefully float the Cabernet on top by pouring it gently over the back of a spoon.

Garnish with an orange twist by expressing the citrus oils over the drink and dropping it in.

MEADOW BREEZE

A perfect sipper for lounging in the sun or enjoying a casual evening with friends, this refreshing drink captures the essence of a gentle summer wind. With floral notes like a meadow in bloom, and a little lemon for a zesty twist, it's Meadow at her effortless, graceful, and elegant best.

4–5 FRESH MINT LEAVES PLUS A FRESH MINT SPRIG, FOR GARNISH

2 OUNCES GIN, SUCH AS ST-GERMAIN

1 OUNCE ELDERFLOWER LIQUEUR

1 OUNCE FRESHLY SQUEEZED LEMON JUICE

½ OUNCE HONEY SYRUP (PAGE 14)

1 OUNCE SODA WATER

LEMON WHEEL, FOR GARNISH

In a cocktail shaker, gently muddle the fresh mint leaves to release their aroma. Add the gin, elderflower liqueur, lemon juice, and honey syrup to the shaker. Fill the shaker with ice cubes and shake vigorously for 10 to 15 seconds to chill and combine. Strain the cocktail into a chilled highball or Collins glass filled with ice cubes. Top up the cocktail with soda water, leaving about ½ inch of space at the top. Give the cocktail a gentle stir to combine the ingredients. Garnish with a lemon wheel and a sprig of fresh mint.

TONY NEGRONI

"Imagine riding in that club car, sipping on a Negroni," Bobby says, admiring the Blue Comet train just before getting whacked. Bobby, we hope you're doing just that, in some better place. We'll even mix it up for you—in our version, with Lillet Blanc and Cocchi Americano. Here's to you, sweet guy.

---

2 OUNCES GIN

1½ OUNCES LILLET BLANC

½ OUNCE COCCHI AMERICANO

ORANGE TWIST, FOR GARNISH

Place a large ice cube in an old-fashioned glass (or rocks glass). In a mixing glass, combine the gin, Lillet Blanc, and Cocchi Americano. Add ice and stir the ingredients for 20 to 30 seconds to chill and combine. Strain the cocktail over the large ice cube in the chilled old-fashioned glass. Garnish with an orange twist by expressing the citrus oils over the drink and dropping it in.

SOPRANOS SANGRIA

A meeting with Tony and his soldiers wouldn't be complete without a bottle of Chianti on the table. After all, a little red wine makes the hit go down more easily. You can use the wine of your choice for our Sopranos Sangria, which gets a little fizz from a healthy glug of prosecco, along with the traditional fruit sangria ingredients. Chill in a pitcher and serve on a hot summer night.

---

1 BOTTLE ITALIAN RED WINE, SUCH AS CHIANTI

½ CUP BRANDY

¼ CUP ORANGE LIQUEUR, SUCH AS TRIPLE SEC

2 TABLESPOONS SIMPLE SYRUP (PAGE 14)

¼ CUP FRESHLY SQUEEZED ORANGE JUICE

¼ CUP POMEGRANATE JUICE

1 CUP CHOPPED MIXED FRUITS, SUCH AS ORANGES, APPLES, BERRIES, AND GRAPES

½ BOTTLE PROSECCO

FRESH MINT LEAVES, FOR GARNISH

CITRUS SLICES, FOR GARNISH

In a large pitcher, combine the red wine, brandy, orange liqueur, simple syrup to taste, orange juice, and pomegranate juice. Stir the mixture to ensure all ingredients are well combined. Add the mixed fruits to infuse the sangria with their flavors. Refrigerate the mixture for at least 1 to 2 hours to allow the flavors to meld and the fruit to absorb the liquid. Before serving, add ice cubes to the pitcher to chill the sangria. Pour the sangria into glasses, filling them about two-thirds full. Top each cocktail with prosecco. Garnish with fresh mint leaves and citrus slices.

SOPRANOS SERENADE MARGARITA

A quintessential margarita is always welcome and easy to shake up—just excellent tequila, lime juice, and triple sec. But when you need to dwell in the land of big men, cool eyes, and steady hands, try our serenade to our favorite Jerseyites. We've replaced triple sec with Grand Marnier for bit of warmth and added a float of sweet Italian wine for . . . well, you know.

---

2 OUNCES REPOSADO TEQUILA

1 OUNCE FRESHLY SQUEEZED LIME JUICE

½ OUNCE AGAVE SYRUP

½ OUNCE GRAND MARNIER

**½ OUNCE ITALIAN SWEET RED WINE,
SUCH AS MARSALA**

LIME WHEEL, FOR GARNISH

Fill a cocktail shaker with ice. Add the reposado tequila, lime juice, agave syrup, and Grand Marnier. Shake the ingredients vigorously for 10 to 15 seconds to chill and combine. Strain the cocktail into a rocks glass filled with ice. Carefully float the Italian sweet red wine on top of the drink by pouring it gently over the back of a spoon, creating a layered effect. Garnish with a lime wheel for an attractive finishing touch.

TONY'S RUM & COKE

Coke can settle an upset stomach, as Carmela tells Tony, and it's a good mixer, too. Once he's recovered from his sickness, he might appreciate this lively rum and Coke with a splash of amaro and a squeeze of lime juice for pucker. Paulie and Silvio might want to have one of these, too—to brace them up before they have to whack an old friend.

---

2 OUNCES DARK RUM

1 OUNCE AMARO

½ OUNCE FRESHLY SQUEEZED LIME JUICE

4 OUNCES COLA

LIME WHEEL, LIME SLICE, FOR GARNISH

FRESH MINT LEAVES, FOR GARNISH

Fill a highball glass with ice cubes. Add the dark rum, amaro, and lime juice. Top off the cocktail with cola. Give the cocktail a gentle stir to combine the ingredients. Garnish with a lime wheel, a lime slice, and fresh mint leaves.

SOPRANOS SUMMER SIPPER

Summer in Jersey means cruising on *The Stugots*, the deck at Whitecaps (for a hot minute), or even just sitting in lawn chairs in the backyard. Instead of a beer, mix up our Sopranos Summer Sipper, a spritz with a bit of wine, a bit of lemon soda, a bit of lemon juice, and a bit of simple syrup. Pour it over a goblet of ice, sit back in that lawn chair, and enjoy.

---

2 OUNCES CHIANTI

**1 OUNCE ITALIAN LEMON SODA
(OR REGULAR LEMON SODA)**

½ OUNCE FRESHLY SQUEEZED LEMON JUICE

½ OUNCE SIMPLE SYRUP (PAGE 14)

LEMON WHEEL, FOR GARNISH

FRESH BASIL SPRIG, FOR GARNISH

Fill a wineglass with ice cubes. Add the Chianti to the glass for the base. Pour in the lemon soda, lemon juice, and the simple syrup. Stir the ingredients gently to combine. Garnish with a lemon wheel for a citrusy touch and a sprig of fresh basil for a refreshing aroma.

TONY'S NIGHTCAP

A nightcap or a pick-me-up is always welcome—the time of day depends on whether the addition of a little coffee will jolt you awake at bedtime. Winding down at the end of a long day, the big guy will appreciate our nightcap. We've added amaretto for an Italian flair and bourbon, Tony's favorite spirit, to a delicious combination of coffee, cream, and spicy, warming cinnamon spirit.

---

2 OUNCES BOURBON WHISKEY

1 OUNCE AMARETTO LIQUEUR

1 OUNCE COLD-BREW COFFEE, CHILLED

½ OUNCE CINNAMON SYRUP (PAGE 17)

1 OUNCE HEAVY CREAM

CINNAMON STICK OR FRESHLY GRATED CINNAMON, FOR GARNISH

Fill a rocks glass with ice cubes. Add the bourbon whiskey, amaretto liqueur, cold-brew coffee, and cinnamon syrup. Add the heavy cream. Stir the ingredients gently in the glass to combine. Garnish with a cinnamon stick or a sprinkle of freshly grated cinnamon.

CELEBRATIONS AND OCCASIONS

The happy, the sad, the murderous—we've got a drink for every *Sopranos* event. Carmela's going to Paris? Check! Tony's in Italy? Check! Dinner at Vesuvio? Try The Martina (page 123)— just keep some ice handy to cool your arm down afterward. Celebrate, or at least sip your sorrows away, with us.

SOPRANOS CELEBRATION

Sometimes celebrations in Tony's world are a little depressing, like Tony and Carmela's eighteenth anniversary celebration. Sometimes they look pretty perfect, like Carmela's living room complete with Christmas tree and AJ's new girlfriend. Either way, a celebration cocktail with a little added hit from Cognac and fresh lemon juice is the perfect drink to help the party along—or to help you drown your sorrows.

1½ OUNCES COGNAC

¾ OUNCE FRESHLY SQUEEZED LEMON JUICE

½ OUNCE SIMPLE SYRUP (PAGE 14)

2½ OUNCES CHAMPAGNE OR SPARKLING WINE, CHILLED

LEMON TWIST, FOR GARNISH

BRANDIED CHERRY, FOR GARNISH

In a cocktail shaker, combine the Cognac, lemon juice, and simple syrup. Fill the shaker with ice. Shake the ingredients vigorously for 10 to 15 seconds to chill and combine. Strain the cocktail into a chilled Champagne flute or coupe glass. Top off the cocktail with chilled Champagne. Garnish with a lemon twist and brandied cherry.

CARMELA IN PARIS

Italy meets America meets France when Carmela and Rosalie take a vacation to the City of Lights. Ro's a little jet-lagged; she loses a glove, and it's cold. But the City of Lights is more beautiful than either of them could have imagined, and with a warming blend of Italian liqueur to take the chill off the famously raw Parisian weather, Carmela and Ro might never be ready to leave France.

---

1 OUNCE COGNAC

1 OUNCE AMARETTO LIQUEUR

½ OUNCE ORANGE LIQUEUR

ORANGE TWIST, FOR GARNISH

In a mixing glass, combine the Cognac, amaretto liqueur, and orange liqueur. Fill the mixing glass with ice. Stir the ingredients for 20 to 30 seconds to chill and combine. Strain the cocktail into a chilled cocktail glass. Garnish with a twist of orange peel by expressing the citrus oils over the drink and dropping it in.

LIMONCELLO ROYALE

When Junior smooshes a lemon meringue pie (with one piece missing) into Bobbi's face, she might have gotten a little taste of lemon, though she'd probably rather have had her dessert on a plate with a fork. Or perhaps she would have liked her lemon from limoncello, the Italian liqueur made from lemon peel. After she washes her face, she could have our lemony royale, made with either prosecco or Champagne. Or she could throw it in Junior's face. That might be even more satisfying.

1 OUNCE GIN

½ OUNCE LIMONCELLO

½ OUNCE FRESHLY SQUEEZED LEMON JUICE

¼ OUNCE SIMPLE SYRUP (PAGE 14)

2 OUNCES PROSECCO OR CHAMPAGNE

LEMON TWIST, FOR GARNISH

Fill a cocktail shaker with ice. Add the gin, limoncello, lemon juice, and simple syrup. Shake the ingredients vigorously for 10 to 15 seconds to chill and combine. Strain the cocktail into a Champagne flute. Top it off with the prosecco or Champagne. Garnish with a lemon twist for added aroma and presentation.

THE MARTINA

Martinis. Chilled, pearly sophistication. Just like Benny plunging
Artie's hand into a pot of boiling marinara sauce. Benny should have
taken Artie up on his offer of a Martina during the Vesuvio dinner
instead. Who knows, maybe Artie could have made that Martina
Sopranos-style, with whiskey instead of gin. After all, nothing
screams sophistication like third-degree hand burns.

---

2 OUNCES BRANDY OR COGNAC

1 OUNCE SWEET VERMOUTH

½ OUNCE SIMPLE SYRUP (PAGE 14)

3 DASHES ORANGE BITTERS

LEMON TWIST, FOR GARNISH

In a mixing glass, combine the brandy or Cognac, sweet vermouth,
simple syrup, and orange bitters. Fill the glass with ice and stir
for 20 to 30 seconds to chill and combine. Strain into a chilled
cocktail glass. Garnish with an lemon twist.

VESUVIO MARTINI

Vesuvio is a bombed-out shell, thunderstorm refuge, site of a boiling marinara-hand collision. Artie's beloved restaurant—and Tony's, too. Here, a chance to raise a glass to that comforting place full of pasta, wine, and grappa. We've doused a martini with limoncello and thrown in a match of triple sec—all the better to set a spectacular explosion.

1½ OUNCES COGNAC

2 OUNCES LIMONCELLO

1 OUNCE VODKA

½ OUNCE TRIPLE SEC OR COINTREAU

½ OUNCE FRESHLY SQUEEZED LEMON JUICE

LEMON TWIST OR WHEEL, FOR GARNISH

Chill a martini glass by filling it with ice and letting it sit while you prepare the cocktail. In a cocktail shaker, combine the Cognac, limoncello, vodka, triple sec, and lemon juice. Fill the cocktail shaker with ice cubes. Shake the ingredients vigorously for 10 to 15 seconds to chill and combine. Empty the ice from the glass, then strain the cocktail into the chilled martini glass. Garnish with either a lemon twist or lemon wheel.

LUXURY LOUNGE

Channel some old Hollywood glamour in a shout-out to Chris and Little Carmine's West Coast trip, where the swag is easy to get, and the Luxury Lounge access is not. We use chilled sparkling wine as a base here, with a dash of bitters for complexity and a bit of simple syrup for sweetness. Add a Luxardo cherry garnish for a drink that screams class—and parking lot punches.

---

4 OUNCES CHILLED CHAMPAGNE OR SPARKLING WINE

**½ OUNCE COINTREAU, TRIPLE SEC,
OR OTHER ORANGE LIQUEUR**

½ OUNCE SIMPLE SYRUP (PAGE 14)

**2 DASHES AROMATIC BITTERS,
SUCH AS ANGOSTURA**

LEMON TWIST, FOR GARNISH

LUXARDO CHERRY, FOR GARNISH

In a chilled Champagne flute, combine the chilled Champagne, Cointreau, simple syrup, and aromatic bitters. Gently stir the ingredients in the flute to combine. Garnish with a lemon twist and a Luxardo cherry.

BOURBON RICKEY

When Tony derisively tells Chris to "go have a lime rickey," he's probably thinking of the old-time soda fountain drink made of lime juice, sugar syrup, and seltzer. Because Chris is trying to stay sober, he might want to avoid our version, which turns the mocktail into a cocktail with the addition of bourbon. Bottoms up!

---

2 OUNCES BOURBON

1 OUNCE FRESHLY SQUEEZED LIME JUICE

½ OUNCE SIMPLE SYRUP (PAGE 14)

3 OUNCES CLUB SODA OR SPARKLING WATER

LIME WEDGE OR WHEEL, FOR GARNISH

Fill a highball glass with ice cubes. Add the bourbon, lime juice, and simple syrup. Top off the cocktail with club soda. Gently stir to mix the ingredients. Garnish with a lime wedge or wheel.

FURIO'S MARTINI

Furio will be whisked right back to that Naples olive oil farm he remembers so fondly if he tries this infused martini. We like the extra texture and rich, savory flavor the olive oil pour adds to this classic cocktail. A bit unusual? Perhaps. Delicious? Most definitely.

2 OUNCES GIN

½ OUNCE DRY VERMOUTH

½ OUNCE EXTRA-VIRGIN OLIVE OIL

**2 DASHES AROMATIC BITTERS,
SUCH AS ANGOSTURA**

LEMON TWIST OR OLIVES, FOR GARNISH

In a mixing glass, combine the gin, dry vermouth, olive oil, and aromatic bitters to infuse the cocktail. Add ice and stir the ingredients gently for 20 to 30 seconds to chill and combine. The olive oil may not fully mix but will add texture to the cocktail. Strain into a chilled coupe or martini glass. Garnish with a lemon twist or an olive or two.

THE STUGOTS

Cement block, check. Chains, check. Hidden gun stashed in a fish, check. Tony's leisurely day on the water might not look like everybody else's. Still, whether he's piloting *The Stugots* or Chucky Signore's runabout boat, Tony can still enjoy the Jersey waters, especially with our summer drink in one hand. Coconut cream, pineapple juice, and citrus finishers get a welcome wake-up from a silver tequila shot. Add a festive pineapple wedge and a cherry garnish, and be sure to wrap that chain around the body tight.

1½ OUNCES SILVER TEQUILA

½ OUNCE TRIPLE SEC OR
ORANGE LIQUEUR

1 OUNCE COCONUT CREAM

1 OUNCE PINEAPPLE JUICE

½ OUNCE FRESHLY SQUEEZED LIME JUICE

½ OUNCE SIMPLE SYRUP (PAGE 14)

PINEAPPLE WEDGE, FOR GARNISH

MARASCHINO CHERRY, FOR GARNISH

In a cocktail shaker, combine the silver tequila, triple sec, coconut cream, pineapple juice, lime juice, and simple syrup. Add a handful of ice cubes to the shaker. Shake vigorously for 15 to 20 seconds to chill and combine. Strain the shaken cocktail into a rocks glass filled with ice. Garnish with a pineapple wedge and a maraschino cherry.

ITALIAN SOUR

The sour, a very American drink, gets our Italian twist with Malfy gin for a citrusy flavor, and Aperol, a bittersweet Italian liqueur. Sours can be made without egg white, but we like to add one to foam up and cushion the citrus shiver. Tony and Carmela's slushy, gray-cement world is far away from the sunbaked cliffs and wrinkled blue sea of the Amalfi Coast, but maybe you can find a little Italian sunshine when you mix this one up in your own kitchen and sip it on the front porch.

1½ OUNCES MALFY GIN

1 OUNCE APEROL

¾ OUNCE FRESHLY SQUEEZED LEMON JUICE

½ OUNCE SIMPLE SYRUP (PAGE 14)

1 EGG WHITE

LEMON WHEEL OR TWIST, FOR GARNISH

CHERRY, FOR GARNISH

In a cocktail shaker, combine the Malfy gin, Aperol, lemon juice, simple syrup, and egg white. Dry shake (shake without ice) the ingredients vigorously for 10 to 15 seconds to froth the egg white. After the dry shake, add ice to the shaker. Shake the mixture again, this time with ice, for another 10 to 15 seconds to chill the cocktail and further froth the egg white. Strain the cocktail into a chilled coupe glass. Garnish with a lemon wheel or twist and a cherry.

APERITIVO MULE

Tony might want to remember his trip to Naples with Paulie and Chris by mixing up our Italian-stye mule, either in the usual copper mug or a highball glass. The vodka will help the Commendatori forget the fight with Annalisa Zucca, even as the bitter, bright Aperol reminds him of Italian sunshine—and Italian mobsters.

---

2 OUNCES VODKA

1 OUNCE APEROL

½ OUNCE FRESHLY SQUEEZED LIME JUICE

3 OUNCES GINGER BEER

ORANGE SLICE, FOR GARNISH

FRESH MINT SPRIG, FOR GARNISH

Fill a copper mug or highball glass with ice cubes. Add the vodka to the mug. Pour in the Aperol for a bright and slightly bitter flavor. Add the lime juice. Top off the cocktail with ginger beer to your preferred level. Give the cocktail a gentle stir to combine the ingredients. Garnish with an orange slice for a citrusy touch and a sprig of fresh mint.

WHACKED SPRITZ

So many chances to get whacked, so little time. And so much blood cleanup. This crimson-colored drink will sustain you. Homemade raspberry syrup is easy to make (combine raspberries, water, and sugar, boil, and strain) and gorgeous to look at when you're done. Blood-red and glowing, the syrup will turn your limoncello spritz into something special, with delicious fruit flavor.

---

1 OUNCE LIMONCELLO

3 OUNCES PROSECCO OR SPARKLING WINE

½ OUNCE RASPBERRY SYRUP (PAGE 17)

1 OUNCE CLUB SODA

FRESH RASPBERRIES, FOR GARNISH

LEMON TWIST OR WHEEL, FOR GARNISH

Fill a wine or spritz glass with ice cubes. Add the limoncello, prosecco, raspberry syrup, and club soda. Stir the ingredients gently in the glass to combine. Garnish with fresh raspberries and a lemon twist or wheel.

AMALFI COAST SOUR

Three Jersey mobsters would be right at home on the Amalfi Coast with this sour in their hands. Italian gin (made with Amalfi lemon peel) and fresh lemon juice provide pucker, simple syrup sweetens it up, and a slug of olive oil adds richness and texture. Tony can offer Furio one, too, to ease the future homesickness.

2 OUNCES MALFY GIN

¾ OUNCE FRESHLY SQUEEZED LEMON JUICE

½ OUNCE SIMPLE SYRUP (PAGE 14)

¼ OUNCE EXTRA-VIRGIN OLIVE OIL

LEMON WHEEL OR TWIST, FOR GARNISH

In a cocktail shaker, combine the Malfy gin, lemon juice, simple syrup, and olive oil. Fill the cocktail shaker with ice cubes. Shake the ingredients vigorously for 10 to 15 seconds to chill and combine. Strain the cocktail into a rocks glass over fresh ice. Garnish with a lemon wheel or twist.

CLASSICS

No need to alter these gold standards—just mix as they've always been mixed and enjoy while thinking of our own classic mobster. Even the Apple Martini (page 145) made the list— *especially* the Apple Martini. It's a classic now, didn't you know?

APPLE MARTINI

Tina's Apple Martini is the perfect club drink, especially when you're wearing a giant mink—sorry, *fox*—coat. We've mixed up a classic one here, with Sour Apple Pucker, vodka, and Cointreau. No need to mess with perfection. Adriana can even throw this sweet drink in her maid of honor's face for flirting with Christopher.

---

2 OUNCES VODKA

1 OUNCE DEKUYPER SOUR APPLE PUCKER

½ OUNCE COINTREAU

½ OUNCE FRESHLY SQUEEZED LEMON JUICE

APPLE SLICE OR LEMON TWIST, FOR GARNISH

In a cocktail shaker, combine the vodka, Sour Apple Pucker, Cointreau, and lemon juice. Fill the shaker with ice. Shake vigorously for 20 to 30 seconds. Strain into a chilled martini glass. Garnish with apple slices or a lemon twist.

THE REVOLVER

Could there be a better cocktail for New Jersey's capos? This coffee-flavored variation of a Manhattan gets a warm nuttiness from coffee liqueur, which blends deliciously with orange bitters. Load this cocktail into your clip and pull the trigger to get good and properly whacked.

---

2 OUNCES BOURBON OR RYE WHISKEY

½ OUNCE COFFEE LIQUEUR, SUCH AS KAHLÚA

2 DASHES ORANGE BITTERS

ORANGE TWIST OR SLICE, FOR GARNISH

In a mixing glass, filled with ice, combine the bourbon, coffee liqueur, and orange bitters. Stir the ingredients in the mixing glass for 20 to 30 seconds to chill and combine. Strain the cocktail into a chilled coupe glass. Garnish with an orange twist.

BLACK MANHATTAN

A classic Manhattan is mixed with whiskey, vermouth, and bitters. A Black Manhattan is even tastier, if that's possible. Adding Amaro Averna in place of the vermouth lends a bitter note rather than the sweetness of a typical Manhattan. Consider mixing one of these as a love note to the Italian heritage of our most favorite mobsters.

2 OUNCES BOURBON OR RYE WHISKEY

1 OUNCE AMARO AVERNA

2 DASHES AROMATIC BITTERS, SUCH AS ANGOSTURA

ORANGE TWIST OR CHERRY, FOR GARNISH

In a mixing glass, filled with ice, combine the bourbon, Amaro Averna, and aromatic bitters. Stir the ingredients for 20 to 30 seconds to chill and combine. Strain the cocktail into a chilled coupe glass. Garnish with an orange twist or cherry.

RUSTY NAIL

Carmela might be in a better mood if she actually accepted the Rusty Nail Tony B offers to make her. This classic drink can take the edge off any party stress. Blending whiskey with Drambuie makes a strong alcohol combo with just a hint of spicy sweetness. Come on, Carmela—take a drink.

2 OUNCES SCOTCH WHISKY

½ OUNCE DRAMBUIE

LEMON TWIST OR WEDGE, FOR GARNISH

Fill a rocks glass with ice cubes. Add the Scotch whisky and Drambuie. Stir the ingredients gently in the glass to combine. Garnish with a lemon twist or wedge.

ABOUT THE CONTRIBUTORS

SARAH GUALTIERI (RECIPES AND PHOTOGRAPHY) is a Long Island–based recipe developer and photographer. She works with beverage brands to develop cocktails and mocktails for the home bartender. Sarah's passion for mixology stems from her love of exploring different ingredients and their potential to elevate the drinking experience. Beyond mixology, she shares her culinary adventures on social media, inspiring others to try new recipes and techniques in their own kitchens.

EMMA CARLSON BERNE (TEXT) is an author who often writes about food, history, and pop culture. Her other books include *The Ultimate Driving Book*, as well as the thrillers *Never Let You Go* and *Still Waters*. Emma lives in Cincinnati. More on Emma can be found at emmacarlsonberne.com.

INDEX

A

Amalfi Coast Sour, 140–141
amaretto
    The Bada Bing!, 52–53
    The Big Guy, 86–87
    Carmela in Paris, 118–119
    The Hitman, 38–39
    Italian American, 96–97
    Tony's Nightcap, 112–113
amaretto cream, 44–45
Amaro
    Black Manhattan, 148–149
    Espresso and Tonic, 48–49
    Italian Espresso Martini,
    44–45
    Italian Highball, 28–29
    Tony's Rum and Coke,
    108–109
Americano Sopranos, 94–95
Angostura bitters
    The Big Guy, 86–87
    Black Manhattan, 148–149
    Cognac Capo Sangaree, 30–31
    Furio's Martini, 130–131
    Grappa Sour, 84–85
    Italian American, 96–97
    Italian Highball, 28–29
    Tony's Old-Fashioned, 82–83
    Whacked Long Island, 40–41
Aperol
    Aperitivo Mule, 136–137
    Italian Sour, 134–135
    Sopranos Speakeasy Sour,
    98–99
apple brandy, 60–61
Apple Martini, 144–145
aromatic bitters
    The Big Guy, 86–87
    Black Manhattan, 148–149

Cognac Capo Sangaree, 30–31
Furio's Martini, 130–131
Grappa Sour, 84–85
Italian American, 96–97
Italian Highball, 28–29
Luxury Lounge, 126–127
Smoked Scotch, 36–37
Tony's Old-Fashioned, 82–83
Whacked Long Island, 40–41
Atlantic City Margarita, 56–57
Averna, Amaro, 148–149

B

The Bada Bing!, 52–53
Bad Blood, 34–35
Barspoons, 13
The Big Guy, 86–87
bitters. See Angostura Bitters;
    aromatic bitters
blackberry liqueur, 80–81
Black Manhattan, 148–149
blanc lillet, 102–103
blanco tequila, 40–41
blood orange gin, 26–27
Blue Curaçao liqueur
    Atlantic City Margarita, 56–57
    Uncle Junior, 90–91
bourbon
    Americano Sopranos, 94–95
    The Bada Bing!, 52–53
    Bad Blood, 34–35
    The Big Guy, 86–87
    Black Manhattan, 148–149
    Bourbon Rickey, 128–129
    Gold Chain, 92–93
    The Hitman, 38–39
    Italian American, 96–97
    Jersey Storms, 68–69
    New Jersey Summer, 66–67
    The Revolver, 146–147

Sopranos Bourbon Bramble,
    80–81
Sopranos Speakeasy Sour,
    98–99
Tony's Nightcap, 112–113
Whacked Whiskey Sour,
    24–25
Wild Whiskey Boulevardier,
    78–79
Bourbon Rickey, 128–129
brandy
    Carmela in Paris, 118–119
    Cognac Capo Sangaree, 30–31
    The Jersey Devil, 60–61
    The Martina, 122–123
    Sopranos Celebration,
    116–117
    Sopranos Sangria, 104–105
    Vesuvio Martini, 124–125

C

Cabernet, 98–99
Campari
    Americano Sopranos, 94–95
    New Blood Negroni, 26–27
    Wild Whiskey Boulevardier,
    78–79
Carmela in Paris, 118–119
Carmela's Lillet Spritz, 88–89
champagne
    Limoncello Royale, 120–121
    Luxury Lounge, 126–127
    Sopranos Celebration,
    116–117
chianti
    Sopranos Sangria, 104–105
    Sopranos Summer Sipper,
    110–111
classics, 143–151
    Apple Martini, 144–145

Black Manhattan, 148–149
The Revolver, 146–147
Rusty Nail, 150–151
Cocchi Americano, 102–103
coconut rum, 64–65
coffee liqueur
The Hitman, 38–39
Italian Espresso Martini,
44–45
Italian White Russian, 46–47
The Revolver, 146–147
cognac
Carmela in Paris, 118–119
Cognac Capo Sangaree, 30–31
The Martina, 122–123
Sopranos Celebration,
116–117
Sopranos Serenade Margarita,
106–107
Vesuvio Martini, 124–125
Cognac Capo Sangaree, 30–31
Cointreau
Apple Martini, 144–145
Cognac Capo Sangaree, 30–31
Luxury Lounge, 126–127
Vesusio Martini, 124–125
crème de mûre, 80–81
Curaçao liqueur
Atlantic City Margarita, 56–57
Uncle Junior, 90–91

D

dark rum
Jersey Storms, 68–69
Tony's Rum and Coke,
108–109
Dekuyper Sour Apple Pucker,
144–145
Drambuie, 150–151
dry vermouth
Furio's Martini, 130–131
Jersey Tomato Martini, 58–59

E

elderflower liqueur
Carmela's Lillet Spritz, 88–89
Meadow Breeze, 100–101
Espresso and Tonic, 48–49
event drinks, 115–141
Amalfi Coast Sour, 140–141
Aperitivo Mule, 136–137
Bourbon Rickey, 128–129
Carmela in Paris, 118–119
Furio's Martini, 130–131
Italian Sour, 134–135
Limoncello Royale, 120–121
Luxury Lounge, 126–127
The Martina, 122–123
Sopranos Celebration,
116–117
The Stugots, 132–133
Vesusio Martini, 124–125
Whacked Spritz, 138–139

F

family favorites, 75–113
Americano Sopranos, 94–95
The Big Guy, 86–87
Carmela's Lillet Spritz, 88–89
Gold Chain, 92–93
Grappa Sour, 84–85
Italian American, 96–97
Meadow Breeze, 100–101
Sopranos Bourbon Bramble,
80–81
Sopranos Martini, 76–77
Sopranos Sangria, 104–105
Sopranos Serenade Margarita,
106–107
Sopranos Speakeasy Sour,
98–99
Sopranos Summer Sipper,
110–111
Tony Negroni, 102–103
Tony's Nightcap, 112–113
Tony's Old-Fashioned, 82–83
Tony's Rum and Coke,
108–109
Uncle Junior, 90–91
Wild Whiskey Boulevardier,
78–79
Fernet-Branca, 92–93
Furio's Martini, 130–131

G

Garden State Punch, 70–71
gin
Amalfi Coast Sour, 140–141
Furio's Martini, 130–131
Italian Sour, 134–135
Jersey Tomato Martini, 58–59
Limoncello Royale, 120–121
Meadow Breeze, 100–101
New Blood Negroni, 26–27
Pine Barrens Tonic, 62–63
Tony Negroni, 102–103
Uncle Junior, 90–91
Whacked Long Island, 40–41
glassware, 13
Gold Chain, 92–93
Grand Marnier
Cognac Capo Sangaree, 30–31
Sopranos Serenade Magarita,
106–107
Grappa Sour, 84–85

H

The Hitman, 38–39

I

Italian American, 96–97
Italian Espresso Martini, 44–45
Italian Highball, 28–29
Italian lemon soda, 110–111
Italian red wine, 104–105
Italian Sour, 134–135
Italian White Russian, 46–47

J

The Jersey Devil, 60–61
Jersey Shore Sunrise, 72–73
Jersey Storms, 68–69
Jersey Tomato Martini, 58–59
Jiggers, 13

K

Kahlúa
    The Hitman, 38–39
    Italian Espresso Martini,
    44–45
    Italian White Russian, 46–47
    The Revolver, 146–147

L

light rum, 40–41
Lillet
    Carmela's Lillet Spritz, 88–89
    Mafia Martini, 32–33
Lillet Blanc, 102–103
Limoncello Royale, 120–121
Luxardo
    The Bada Bing!, 52–53
    Mafia Martini, 32–33
Luxury Lounge, 126–127

M

mafia hits, 21–49
    Bad Blood, 34–35
    Cognac Capo Sangaree, 30–31
    Espresso and Tonic, 48–49
    The Hitman, 38–39
    Italian Espresso Martini,
    44–45
    Italian Highball, 28–29
    Italian White Russia, 46–47
    Mafia Martini, 32–33
    New Blood Negroni,
    26–27
    Paulie Walnuts Old-Fashioned,
    22–23
    Rise and Crime, 42–43
    Smoked Scotch, 36–37

Whacked Long Island, 40–41
Whacked Whiskey Sour,
24–25
Mafia Martini, 32–33
Malfy blood orange gin, 26–27
Malfy gin
    Amalfi Coast Sour, 140–141
    Italian Sour, 134–135
Maraschino
    The Bada Bing!, 52–53
    Mafia Martini, 32–33
Marsala, 106–107
The Martina, 122–123
Meadow Breeze, 100–101
Muddlers, 13

N

New Blood Negroni, 26–27
New Jersey classics, 51–73
    Atlantic City Margarita, 56–57
    The Bada Bing!, 52–53
    Garden State Punch, 70–71
    The Jersey Devil, 60–61
    Jersey Shore Sunrise, 72–73
    Jersey Storms, 68–69
    Jersey Tomato Martini, 58–59
    New Jersey Summer, 66–67
    Pine Barrens Highball, 54–55
    Pine Barrens Tonic, 62–63
    Whitecaps Punch, 64–65
New Jersey Summer, 66–67

O

orange bitters
    Bad Blood, 34–35
    The Hitman, 38–39
    The Martina, 122–123
    Tony's Old-Fashioned, 82–83
orange liqueur
    Apple Martini, 144–145
    Atlantic City Margarita, 56–57
    Carmela in Paris, 118–119
    Cognac Capo Sangaree, 30–31
    Luxury Lounge, 126–127
    The Revolver, 146–147
    Sopranos Martini, 76–77

Sopranos Sangria, 104–105
The Stugots, 132–133
Vesusio Martini, 124–125
Whacked Long Island, 40–41

P

Paulie Walnuts Old-Fashioned,
    22–23
Pine Barrens Highball, 54–55
Pine Barrens Tonic, 62–63
port wine, 30–31
prosecco
    Limoncello Royale, 120–121
    Sopranos Sangria, 104–105
    Whacked Spritz, 138–139

R

red wine
    Americano Sopranos, 94–95
    Cognac Capo Sangaree, 30–31
    The Martina, 122–123
    New Blood Negroni, 26–27
    Sopranos Sangria, 104–105
    Sopranos Serenade Margarita,
    106–107
    Sopranos Speakeasy Sour,
    98–99
    Sopranos Summer Sipper,
    110–111
    Wild Whiskey Boulevardier,
    78–79
Rémy Martin cognac, 30–31
reposado tequila, 106–107
The Revolver, 146–147
Rise and Crime, 42–43
rum
    Jersey Storms, 68–69
    Tony's Rum and Coke,
    108–109
    Whacked Long Island, 40–41
    Whitecaps Punch, 64–65
Rusty Nail, 150–151
rye whiskey
    Americano Sopranos, 94–95
    The Bada Bing!, 52–53
    Black Manhattan, 148–149

The Revolver, 146–147
Wild Whiskey Boulevardier,
78–79

S

Sambuca
    Italian White Russian, 46–47
    Rise and Crime, 42–43
scotch
    The Big Guy, 86–87
    Rusty Nail, 150–151
    Smoked Scotch, 36–37
    Tony's Old-Fashioned, 82–83
shakers, 13
silver tequila
    Atlantic City Margarita, 56–57
    The Stugots, 132–133
Smoked Scotch, 36–37
Sopranos Bourbon Bramble,
    80–81
Sopranos Celebration, 116–117
Sopranos Martini, 76–77
Sopranos Sangria, 104–105
Sopranos Serenade Margarita,
    106–107
Sopranos Speakeasy Sour, 98–99
Sopranos Summer Sipper,
    110–111
sparkling wine
    Luxury Lounge, 126–127
    Sopranos Celebration,
    116–117
    Whacked Spritz, 138–139
St. Germain elderflower liqueur
    Carmela's Lillet Spritz, 88–89
    Meadow Breeze, 100–101
Strainers, 13
The Stugots, 132–133
sweet red wine, 106–107
sweet vermouth
    Americano Sopranos, 94–95
    The Martina, 122–123
    New Blood Negroni, 26–27
    Wild Whiskey Boulevardier,
    78–79
syrups, 14–17

T

tequila
    Atlantic City Margarita, 56–57
    Sopranos Serenade Margarita,
    106–107
    The Stugots, 132–133
    Whacked Long Island, 40–41
Tony Negroni, 102–103
Tony's Nightcap, 112–113
Tony's Old-Fashioned, 82–83
Tony's Rum and Coke, 108–109
triple sec
    Atlantic City Margarita, 56–57
    Cognac Capo Sangaree, 30–31
    Luxury Lounge, 126–127
    Sopranos Martini, 76–77
    Sopranos Sangria, 104–105
    The Stugots, 132–133
    Vesusio Martini, 124–125
    Whacked Long Island, 40–41

U

Uncle Junior, 90–91

V

vermouth
    Americano Sopranos, 94–95
    Furio's Martini, 130–131
    Jersey Tomato Martini, 58–59
    The Martina, 122–123
    New Blood Negroni, 26–27
    Wild Whiskey Boulevardier,
    78–79
    Vesusio Martini, 124–125
vodka
    Aperitivo Mule, 136–137
    Apple Martini, 144–145
    Garden State Punch, 70–71
    Italian Espresso Martini,
    44–45
    Italian White Russian, 46–47
    The Jersey Devil, 60–61
    Jersey Shore Sunrise, 72–73

Jersey Tomato Martini, 58–59
Mafia Martini, 32–33
Vesusio Martini, 124–125

W

Whacked Long Island, 40–41
Whacked Spritz, 138–139
Whacked Whiskey Sour, 24–25
whiskey, 150–151
    Americano Sopranos, 94–95
    The Bada Bing!, 52–53
    The Big Guy, 86–87
    Black Manhattan, 148–149
    Jersey Storms, 68–69
    Paulie Walnuts Old-Fashioned,
    22–23
    Pine Barrens Highball, 54–55
    The Revolver, 146–147
    Rusty Nail, 150–151
    Smoked Scotch, 36–37
    Sopranos Martini, 76–77
    Tony's Nightcap, 112–113
    Tony's Old-Fashioned, 82–83
    Whacked Long Island, 40–41
    Whacked Whiskey Sour,
    24–25
    Wild Whiskey Boulevardier,
    78–79
whiskey bourbon, 40–41
Whitecaps Punch, 64–65
white rum, 64–65
white wine
    Carmela's Lillet Spritz, 88–89
    Furio's Martini, 130–131
    Jersey Tomato Martini, 58–59
    Limoncello Royale, 120–121
    Luxury Lounge, 126–127
    Mafia Martini, 32–33
    Sopranos Celebration,
    116–117
    Sopranos Sangria, 104–105
    Tony Negroni, 102–103
    Whacked Spritz, 138–139
Wild Whiskey Boulevardier,
    78–79

INSIGHT
EDITIONS

an imprint of Insight Editions
P.O. Box 3088
San Rafael, CA 94912
www.weldonowen.com

CEO Raoul Goff
VP Publisher Roger Shaw
Publishing Director Katie Killebrew
Executive Editor Edward Ash-Milby
VP Creative Chrissy Kwasnik
Art Director Megan Sinead Bingham
Production Designer Jean Hwang
VP Manufacturing Alix Nicholaeff
Sr Production Manager Joshua Smith
Sr Production Manager, Subsidiary Rights Lina s Palma-Temena

Photography and Prop Stylist Sarah Gultieri

Cover Illustration by Adam Raiti

Weldon Owen would also like to thank Crystal Erickson and Mary Cassells.

ISBN: 979-8-88663-567-6

Manufactured in China by Insight Editions
10 9 8 7 6 5 4 3 2 1

Insight Editions, in association with Roots of Peace, will plant two trees for each tree used in the
manufacturing of this book. Roots of Peace is an internationally renowned humanitarian organization
dedicated to eradicating land mines worldwide and converting war-torn lands into productive farms
and wildlife habitats. Roots of Peace will plant two million fruit and nut trees in Afghanistan and provide
farmers there with the skills and support necessary for sustainable land use.